SCENES FROM THE PAST

RAILWAYS OF THE HIGH

BUXTON

—— ENGINES & MEN ——

Buxton, 1950's. The site of the original LNWR shed was ultimately used to locate the diesel maintenance depot. Prior to this, the sidings had seen a variety of uses, including the storage of carriages, vans etc.,In its finalyears before redevelopment, the site saw more of the kind of activity seen here,with the parachute water column being used by train engines of through freight workings requiring to replenish their supply. The engines would be detached form their trains at Buxton No 1 signal box for this purpose and here we see LNWR 0-8-0 No **48942** with Driver Jim Murfin in charge, waiting to rejoin its train. This was a time consuming procedure, overcome eventually by erecting a water column at No 1 box. *L.M.Hobdey*

J.M.BENTLEY

Copyright © 1995 Foxline Publishing and J.M. Bentley
ISBN 1 870119 38 X
All rights reserved
Edited by Gregory K. Fox
Typeset by Bill Rear, Johnstown, Wrexham
Printed by the Amadeus Press, Huddersfield

Published by Foxline Publishing
32, Urwick Road, Romiley, Stockport. SK6 3JS

Driver Harry Moss and Fireman David
Plant pose at the side of No **48744,** the
last steam engine to depart from Buxton
shed on the 2nd March 1968.

J.M.Bentley

RAILWAYS OF THE HIGH PEAK
BUXTON - ENGINES & MEN

Introduction

For two companies whose arrival in the town was within days of each other, (so far as official openings were concerned), the respective developments and priorities in the operation of their rival stations differed markedly.

To the Midland Railway Company, Buxton became a depot of strategic importance, as explained in the previous book, (Scenes From The Past:7 *The Railway From Buxton to Bakewell, Matlock & Ambergate*), but to the London & North Western Railway, it was of lesser concern, despite the fact that a desire to compete with the Midland Railway for traffic was the reason for the conception of their station.

In taking over the the Cromford & High Peak Railway, the LNWR had acquired a small engine shed at Ladmanlow, serving the Hopton Top, Bunsall Top section of that line, but they had no direct connection into Buxton other than via Whaley Bridge.

Although the Midland Railway kept a stud of reasonably up to date locomotives at their depot, in the early days the LNWR used their line for 'putting out to grass', various aged and inherited locomotives yet, as the years progressed, and Buxton became as important to the LNWR as it did to the Midland company, there was a change of policy, and the motive power and rolling stock used by the "Premier Line' was the most up to date that company owned, indeed, some coaches were especially designed for the line.

The original LNWR Depot was even more modest than the Midland's establishment; placed where the Diesel Depot now stands, its small two road shed could only accomodate four locomotives, with room for two more in the yard outside. Very scant provision had been made for expansion, this came nearly thirty years later with the opening of the line to Hindlow and Harpur Hill, making a direct connection with the Cromford & High Peak line, and enabling the small depot at Ladmanlow to be closed; its two locomotives were transferred to Buxton shed, as, not long afterwards, was the responsibility for the remainder of the Cromford & High Peak Railway's locomotives.

In preference to enlarging their original Buxton Depot, the LNWR built a new one under Brown Edge, which will be dealt with later in this work. No photographs have come to light showing the original shed and buildings, but a few do exist depicting locomotives standing in the yard; the old structures were dismantled carefully and the stone blocks used to construct the 'coal hole' at the new depot.

The enlargement of the former LNWR Depot was completed in 1935, and enabled the old Midland Depot in Bridge Street to be closed. The closure of any depot and the subsequent transfer of men and work was, and still is, a troublesome business, but when the depots of two, at times bitterly opposed companies are amalgamated, with men on both sides intensely loyal to the old order, trouble just has to ensue.

Buxton MPD n.d; General view of the depot from the top of the water tower.   *J.R.Morten.*

The basic problem at Buxton was that promotion had been much faster on the ex Midland side during the late 1920s and early 1930s than on the former LNWR side, therefore on the Midland side men of 1914-16 seniority were regular drivers, or Passed Firemen (actually doing very little firing at all), whereas men of the same seniority under the North Western regime might have been passed for driving, but were mostly still engaged on firing duties. The practical result of the merger meant rapid promotion for quite a few on the old LNWR side, but a return to firing for many of the ex Midland men; not a happy state of affairs.

More trouble arose when former Midland firemen were put with former LNWR drivers, who had been used to the old LNWR tradition of the fireman doing the oiling round of the locomotive; the 'Midland Railway' men flatly refused to do it, thus many of the old LNWR drivers were seen within the confines of an inside motion for the first time since their firing days.

Route knowledge was the biggest stumbling block however, as no Midland Railway man had ever been over Bibbingtons summit, just as no former LNWR men had ever been past Ashwood Dale, so the link formation was complex to say the least, with the senior men on each side keeping strictly to their own territory, whilst the younger men were taught roads on both sides of the Great Divide, to ensure that as men moved up through the links, on the retirement of the more elderly drivers, of either former 'Midland' or 'LNWR' persuasion, the younger men would be ready and able to take over the link work of either group. The antigonism is now completely gone, yet the old rivalry was still very much in existence up to the early 1960s, showing that old traditions and loyalties died a very slow death.

In this brief history of the LNWR Depots, and 'Men and Engines at Buxton', I have tried to keep everything in chronological order wherever possible so, we commence at the old LNWR Depot in the station yard, pass on to the new depot under Brown Edge, built 1891-92 and then deal with its enlargement in 1934-5. At this point, the LNWR men and engines were, for the first time, fully integrated with the men of the, (then closed), MR, Bridge Street Depot, so quite a few men and engines, previously featured in the last book, which dealt with the MR depot and its men and engines up to 1935 will be seen again, which is only right and proper, and keeps this record of events in its correct perspective.

As for the men of the combined depot, the two sides never really amalgamated properly; rivalry between the two factions was alive and well when your author started (on the railway), in 1957, and it was most interesting to listen to some of the older men, with their bias for the locomotives of their own particular company -nevertheless, this rather unsatisfactory amalgamation produced some very fine drivers from amongst the younger men, who picked up the best points of enginemanship from both sides but not the inherent predjudices of the older men.

Sadly, none of these men remain in service now, so our story is, for the most part history, as is the LNWR Depot under Brown Edge, its untimely demolition much regretted by the present management, as history, (as is it's wont), has repeated itself and the present depot, built on the site of the original LNWR Depot in the station yard, has proved woefully inadequate to house all the locomotives now working in the area.

The Fowler 2-6-4 Tank Engines

Undoubtedly, the most successful and popular locomotives to be used on the passenger services from Buxton were these splendid and reliable machines. The first batches available for the Manchester South passenger traffic obviously went to Longsight, thus enabling Buxton to acquire more L.&Y.Baltic tanks for its rosters, much to the disgust of the staff.

By July 1928, Longsight Depot had No.s.2304, 06, 09, 10, 12, 14, 15, and 16 on its books. No.2304 was probably the very first of the type to work to Buxton. Nos.2323 and 2324 were allocated to Buxton in the summer of 1928, and were tried on all 'our' passenger services, both to Manchester, London Road, and Ashbourne and found to be most successful, so at last it seemed that one class of locomotive could carry out most of the passenger work at the depot. Even so, it was not until 14th August 1929 that the first of 'our' well known batch of Nos.2365 to 2371 was built. Listed below are the dates on which they were built, and allocated to Buxton:

No.2365	14.08.1929
No.2366	27.08.1929
No.2367	02.09.1929
No.2368	06.09.1929
No.2369	11.09.1929
No.2370	16.09.1929
No.2371	19.09.1929

The original two remained at Buxton until about 1934, when No.2381 arrived to replace the Webb 18 inch 0-6-2 tanks on the Ashbourne Services. Nos.2332 and 2340 were allocated to Buxton, Midland depot in 1931, to replace some of the older 2P 4-4-0s, No.2382 arrived 1935-6 for the 1.28 pm Manchester Victoria service.

In 1935-6 the allocation was as follows with regular drivers :

No.2365	Drivers Alf Clayton - J Hooley.	
No.2366	,,	Geo Woodiwiss - W Beresford.
No.2367	,,	R Davies - H Buxton.
No.2368	,,	W Goodwin - G Whitfield.
No.2369	Regular engine for 8.33 am Manchester, London Road.	
No.2370)		
No.2371)	Spare engines.	
No.2381	Geo Boulton 5.40 am Ashbourne engine.	
No.2382	Regular engine for 1.28 pm Manchester Victoria (from Buxton MR station).	

APPENDIX TO THE MINUTES OF MEETING OF LOCAL DEPARTMENTAL COMMITTEE. MOTIVE POWER SECTION BUXTON.

MEETING HELD 21st November 1935.
Minute No.240. Link arrangements for the amalgamated, Midland, Western, Drivers and Firemen, due to the closing of the Midland depot.

Link No.1 (Seniors). Sets of Men 4. Points Worked To : Millers Dale, Peak Forest and Matlock.
Link No.2. Sets of Men 8. Points Worked To : Manchester L/Road, Crewe and Wilmslow.

Link No.2A. Sets of Men 7. Points Worked To : Sheffield, Derby and Manchester Central.

Link No.3. Sets of Men 5. Points Worked To : Manchester London Rd, and Ashbourne.

Link No.3A. Sets of Men 5. Manchester Victoria, Derby and Sheffield.

Link No.4. Sets of Men 8. Points Worked To :Peak Forest, Rowsley and Gowhole.

Link No.5. Sets of Men 8. Points Worked To : Manchester L/Rd, Edgeley and Ashbourne.

Link No.6. Sets of Men 8. Points Worked To : Diggle, Springs Branch (Wigan), Edgeley and Ashbourne.

Link No.7. Sets of Men 7. Points Worked To : Friden, Ladmanlow, Longsight and Edgeley.

Link No.8. Sets of Men 8. Points Worked To : Rowsley, Peak Forest and Gowhole.

Link No.9. Sets of men 8. Points Worked To : Bank engines. Local Shunt.

Link No.10.Sets of Men 7. Points Worked To : Millers Dale, Rowsley and Shed preparations.

Link No.11.Sets of Men 8.   as Link No.10.

The order of Progression for Drivers through the links.

The first 49 of the amalgamated Midland and Western Division Drivers to follow their former link progression ; the remainder of the Drivers and any others registered subsequent to the closure of the Midland depot to be marked up in seniority order in the Links and their order of progression to be as follows : Link 11 to Link 10. Link 10 to 8, thence 7 - 6 - 5 - 4, 3 or 3A, which were considered equal for promotion purposes thence Link 2 or 2A.

1.   Vacancies for Drivers in Link 1 (Seniors) to be filled by men who have passed through the Links as Drivers in the agreed order of progression up to and including No.2 Link, and who then made an application for lighter work for health, etc., reasons or any such drivers who are taken off Main Line work at the behest of the Management. Applications to be considered by the L.D.C.

2.   Vacancies for Drivers in No.9 Link to be filled by men who, before reaching No.2 Link make an application for lighter work for health, etc., reasons, or any such men who are taken off Main Line work at the behest of the Management.

3.   The order of progression for Firemen to be as follows, Link 11 - 10 - 3 - 3A - 2 - 2A - 6 - 7 - 8 - 5 - 4 - 9.

4.   The first 49 Drivers referred to above will follow the following order of progression in order to carry out the above provisions : ex North Western men. Links 5 - 3 - 2, ex Midland men: Links 4 - 3A or 2A - 1 as the men referred to are all booked in these links.

Buxton, 1950's. Platform 1 of the former LNWR sation, known as the Excursion platform, plays host to a stopping train for Manchester London Road in the period shortly before services were taken over by diesel multiple units. These Fowler 2-6-4 tank engines had been the mainstay of the passenger train motive power for over a quarter of a century.
H.Townley.

Cab/Footplate Scene. No.49277.

This cab view, taken from the tender of No.**49277** as she climbs out of Hartington, hauling the Uttoxeter (Pinfold Sidings) to Buxton goods, shows a typical LNWR footplate, never really designed for comfort, indeed, very few steam engines ever were. The driver, Harold Sigley, now passed away, was a man brought up in the traditional LNWR way; he actually started work on the railways just after the amalgamation which led to the formation of the LMS, starting work on Thursday, 10th May 1923. He, like the rest of the LNWR men certainly knew how to handle these locomotives, and could show a young hand, even in the last years of the class, just how little coal it took to make one of these 'Super D's' steam. Starting with less fire than latter-day locomotives would get off the shed with, a couple of rounds would see them blowing off; these were amongst the most economical locomotives we ever knew. Note the single line staff - Hartington to Parsley Hay, erect in its usual place, slid onto the sanding handle on the fireman's side. The bottle on the hob above the firehole door contains Harold's cold tea, a practice no longer seen amongst locomen; cold tea was carried by all, at one time, in either stone, or glass bottles. The regulator is just slightly opened and the reversing wheel back about 1¼ turns, giving just the right blast to keep the thin fire lively, exactly what these locomotives required.

J.M.Bentley

Buxton LNWR. c.1892. Of the early types of motive power, the most reliable was the 'Crewe Goods' 2-4-0, which was to be found all over the system, and most of the passenger and goods work on the Buxton Branch was powered by them. These pictures,taken probably late in 1891, show No.**3032**, in the upper scene with Driver Buxton, and in the lower, with an unknown crew, the elderly driver in the latter also appears on other early photographs. The locomotive was built at Crewe in August 1855, and ran as LNWR, North Eastern Division No.77, becoming LNWR, Northern Division No.477, in August 1857; she was placed on the duplicate list as No.1810 in October 1880, and was finally given a new duplicate list No.3032 in

November 1886; withdrawal took place in May 1894. With only 15¼ inch x 20 inch cylinders, 5 ft diameter driving wheels, and 120 lbs per sq. inch boiler pressure, and no injectors, only axle pumps, life was not easy on the Buxton line for the crews. Braking was by means of six wooden blocks on the tender, there were no brakes at all on the locomotive. Mr Webb fitted a weather board on the tender, to afford a little protection from the elements whilst the locomotive was working over the C.&.H.P.section; running chimney leading there was only the scanty front weatherboard and no roof over the heads of the men on the footplate.

Author's Collection

Buxton Down Sidings. c.1892. During the 1880s, the new 2-4-0T locos designed by F.W.Webb started to appear on surburban services all over the system, replacing the older Allan type locomotives, and Buxton shed eventually got their share. These capable little locomotives soon became the backbone of the motive power stud on the passenger turns from Buxton to Manchester and also, with their small wheels were useful performers on shunting duties. The locomotive seen here No.**2278**, was built at Crewe in October 1877 and probably came to Buxton in the mid 1880s; renumbered 6428 by the LMS in 1928 and 26428 by British Railways in March 1948, and again to 58092 in August 1949, the diminutive engine lasted on the High Peak section until withdrawn in March 1952, with probably 60 years service to this area. Her last sister locomotive had been withdrawn as far back as 1936.

In 1881 the allocation of these locomotives to Buxton was as follows :

No.**2233** Driver William Marsden.	No.**2238** Driver John Warner.
No.**2234** Driver Samuel Needham.	No.**2244** Driver Joseph Browlow.
No.**2235** Spare engine.	No.**1185** Driver James Lawton.
No.**2237** Driver Josiah Mills	

Their diagrams were, in May 1882 as follows : (passengers only) :

No.1. 7.10am Buxton to Manchester, 9.15am Manchester to Buxton, 10.40am Buxton to Manchester, 4.00pm Manchester to Buxton (Sats excepted), 1.30pm Manchester to Buxton (Sats only).

No.2. 7.55am Buxton to Manchester, 1.00pm Manchester to Stockport, 1.30pm Stockport to Alderley, 2.55pm Alderley to Manchester, 4.00pm (Sats only), Manchester to Buxton, 4.55pm Manchester to Buxton (Sats excepted), 9.20pm (Thursday only) Buxton to Stockport, 11.02pm (Thursdays only) Stockport to Buxton, due 11.55pm.

No.3. 5.40pm Buxton to Manchester, 8.15pm Manchester to Buxton, due 9.35pm.

It can be seen from these workings that the passenger work did not amount to a great deal, but it has to be remembered that both Longsight and Whaley Bridge depots had a hand in the work, although the latter depot did not work to Buxton.

Authors Collection.

Buxton c.1890. During the mid 1880s F.W.Webb, as well as producing 3 cylinder compound passenger locomotives, tried his hand with three compound tank locomotives, none of which seemed to do quite what had been expected of them on the services for which they were designed. All three were put into service on the Buxton Branch, two, No.**600**, illustrated here and No.**777**, featured on the next page, were allocated to Buxton for most of their working lives. The first picture shows No.600 standing in the main platform at Buxton, prior to departure for Manchester. She was built at Crewe in June 1887 and, when new, was exhibited alongside the old Crewe Engine 'Columbine', at the entrance to a new park in Crewe, presented to the town by the LNWR Chairman Sir Richard Moon, to celebrate Queen Victoria's Jubilee. No.**600** was a pure, Webb uncoupled 3 cylinder compound, with 5ft 8¼ in diameter driving wheels, two outside 14in x 20in high pressure cylinders and one 26in x 24in low pressure cylinder between the frames. Starting this locomotive from rest at stations like Middlewood and Chapel-en-le-Frith must have sorely tried the drivers' patience, yet the locomotive put in nearly ten years work on the branch and with at the most, the coaching stock fitted with the Webb/Clark chain brake system, put up some quite fast performances on those services. It is interesting to note that these locomotives were given only seven minutes from Buxton to leaving Dove Holes, the same timings allowed for DMU operated services until the arrival of the 'Sprinters' in May 1989, so the 2-2-2-2 compound tanks cannot have been so bad after all. The picture at the top of page 9 shows No.**600** on the turntable at London Road with, it is thought Driver Mottram and Fireman Townley.

C.M.Doncaster.

Manchester, London Road. c.1888-92. A few months after the construction of the compound tank locomotive No.600, Mr Webb turned out his third compound tank locomotive, No.**777**, built specifically for goods work. This rather unusual machine had, in common with all Webb 3 cylinder compounds the inside low pressure cylinder coupled to the leading driving wheels, but the two outside, high pressure cylinders were coupled to four wheels, giving the rare wheel arrangement of 2-2-4-0. How this machine performed on goods trains is shrouded in mystery, but after being on display at Belle Vue, Manchester, she soon found her way, along with No.600 to Buxton, where she worked until late in 1895. No.777 was the very first Crewe locomotive to be fitted with steel buffer beams. The upper picture shows her without a front vacuum pipe, Driver Marcus Weiss on the footplate. The lower illustration, taken after the fitting of the front vacuum pipe is with her regular driver Robert Gartside leaning against the step, in the cab is his regular fireman William Goodwin, who happily lived to a great age, and was able to give very useful information regarding the working of the locomotive. One of its regular turns was the 10.50am slow train from Buxton to Manchester, arriving at London Road 11.56am, it then took its coaching stock to Longsight, arriving there about 12.30pm. Unfortunately No.777 had a rather unfortunate design fault, in the way in which the main steam pipes, leading from the outside high pressure cylinders to the enormous low pressure cylinder between the frames, were jointed to the inside of the main frames behind the high pressure cylinders. On the descent from Buxton these flanged joints would quite often work loose, necessitating a fitters attention at Longsight; unfortunately her arrival there coincided with the start of the engineering staff's dinner time and lots would be drawn as to who would repair No.777. The unfortunate soul(s) would come back to a cold dinner, and for the whole of the engine's life in the area she was known as '*Cold Dinners.*' William Goodwin told of how well this engine managed its work on the banks to Buxton, no doubt aided on starting by the rear four-coupled wheels, against the starting problems suffered by No.600 with its sets of single wheels. Whatever their shortcomings these engines were kept in beautiful condition during their stay at Buxton; it is a pity that more pictures do not exist showing them in action. The other compound tank (not shown, was No.**687**, a small-wheeled 2-2-2-2 type; this did spend some time at Buxton, but also worked from Chelford Depot. No.777 was renumbered No.**1977** in the duplicate list in October 1895, and was transferred away to easier grades about that time; she was finally broken up in November, 1901, one month before No.600 suffered the same fate.

The last of the Jubilees or 5X's to be used on the 08.00 to Manchester Central was No.**45705** *Seahorse*, here seen on the occasion of its clean-up, and nameplate re-fitting. August 15th 1965. *J.M. Bentley*

A view off the top of an 8F's tender looking down the loco yard towards the coaling plant and water tower. *J.M. Bentley*

A general view of the depot from behind the ashpit road, before the removal of the roof. A selection of Ivatt 2-6-0's, 4F 0-6-0's, 8F's and the odd High peak J.94 0-6-0ST's can e seen. *J.R. Morten.*

Towards the end of 1967 the Diesel Electric locomotives that were to replace the 8F's on freight workings started to appear for crew training etc. Here **D213** of Longsight depot is seen arriving at Buxton. The greatest difficulty with these locomotives was their inability to stop loose-coupled trains, after the 8F's which were fitted with probably the finest brake to be found on any locomotive. These machines had the greatest difficulty in holding back anything over 700 tons, and that had to be very carefully managed. Brake fade occurred when the brake was in continuous use for more than 10 or 15 minutes, quite a few hair-raising runs occurred the worst being the run of D375 from Peak Forest to Throstle Nest Junction Manchester, which made the 6 o'clock news. Their cold cabs, more like draught tunnels made them rather unpopular at the side of the Sultzer locomotives which were far better to work on. The one redeeming feature of this particular class was its ability to go on and on, water troubles could be overcome by use of a transfer pump, hand operated, built on steam engine type bogies they rode beautifully. *J.R. Morten.*

Buxton. Site of old Locomotive Depot. c.1894. This interesting photograph was taken during cleaning up operations, just after the demolition of the old shed. The stone from the old buildings was in the process of transference to the new site in the small engineer's wagons, a temporary water tank resting on a stack of sleepers is on the left of the picture. The brand new fencing in the foreground, plus the signal rodding relates to the new bay platform which will, eventually, be known as the Ashbourne bay. The new Webb 2-4-2 tank No.**427** allocated to Buxton as a replacement for one of the compound tanks stands (just), on the turntable. These locomotives worked very well on the passenger services to Manchester, London Road, and Liverpool, Lime Street; they also powered the Ashbourne services until completely replaced by the Webb 18 inch 0-6-2 tanks, whose six coupled driving wheels gave better adhesion on the severe gradients of this area.

Author's Collection

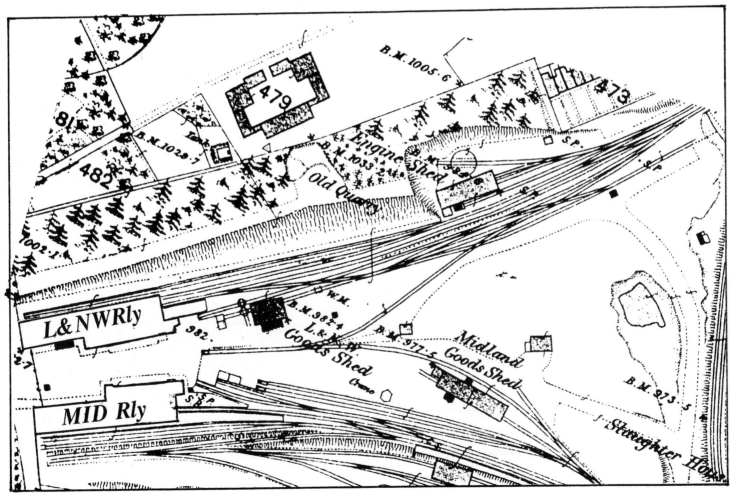

Buxton LNWR. Old Locomotive Depot. c.1894. A Webb 'Coal engine' No.233 poses with its crew in the old shed yard. This very numerous class, along with the even more prolific DX 0-6-0 type, replaced the old Allan, 'Crewe Goods' locomotives all over the LNWR system, except on the C.&.H.P.R. section. Buxton had just two of these locomotives for its small amount of freight work; in 1881 they were :

No.962   Driver Thomas Rubery.
No.2164   Driver William Swann.

Before the days of vacuum braked passenger stock, these locomotives could be, (and were), used on the depot's passenger workings. Although they were much more powerful than the old 'Crewe Goods' type their braking was, alas, just the same, six wooden blocks acting on the tender wheels; they must have spent a great deal of their lives in reverse with steam 'on' to assist in stopping, referred to by LNWR men as "the secret weapon". With these locomotives Drivers Rubery and Swann, as well as others worked what was known as the 'ticket system'. Leaving Buxton on a Monday morning with a goods train heading towards Manchester, on arrival at, say Longsight, they would be given a written order to proceed to Wigan, where they would lodge; the following day the same procedure would apply, with another written notice to proceed northwards, Carlisle being the final destination. The same process operated for the return journey and, if they were very lucky the crew would reach Buxton on Friday evening. Saturday was, then, a free day with pay, but the men were often unlucky and it would be a Saturday arrival back at Buxton. This form of working ceased with the introduction of route knowledge, and route cards, on which men had to sign to the effect that they were thoroughly conversant with the particular routes they regularly worked, so 'route learning' came into being, which cost the company too much money, consequently depots started to work only their own 'regular' routes.   *Authors Collection*

LNWR. Old shed site, Buxton. May 1902. A Webb 18 inch 0-6-2 tank stands on the turntable at the old depot with her crew. These very capable engines completely took over the passenger workings to Manchester, and both freight and passenger work to Ashbourne. The crews greatly appreciated the fact that these locomotives had cast-iron brake blocks and a well protected cab area. During their life on the Manchester passenger turns, the trains became much heavier and faster, as the demands of the Manchester businessmen to live out in the country, and travel quickly into work in a morning were met. No.**14** was built in November 1899, and it can be seen by the circular valve chest covers was fitted with piston valves instead of the -then- more usual slide valves.   *C.H.Eden*

LNWR. Old shed site. c.1901. Driver Tommy Mottram and fireman Robert Davies stand at the side of their immaculate 18 inch 0-6-2 tank No.**1601**, partly turned for the benefit of the photographer, note that even the ash-pan sides are polished.   *C.H.Eden*

Another Buxton 8F No.**48532** is here seen shunting in the LNW Old Yard opposite the diesel depot. This had, prior to the building of the line to Hindlow and the fly-over from that line, been the LNW company's goods yard, its activities being transferred to the new larger yard under Brown Edge in 1892. Latterly it was used to house coaching stock and various departmental vehicles. *J.M. Bentley*

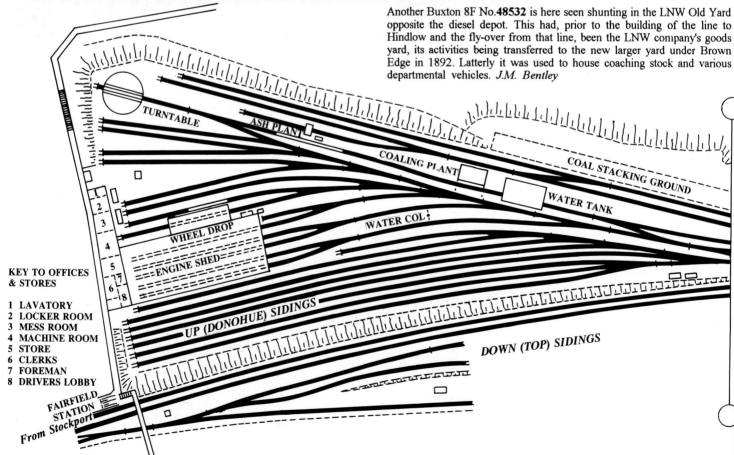

KEY TO OFFICES & STORES

1 LAVATORY
2 LOCKER ROOM
3 MESS ROOM
4 MACHINE ROOM
5 STORE
6 CLERKS
7 FOREMAN
8 DRIVERS LOBBY

TURNTABLE
ASH PLANT
COALING PLANT
COAL STACKING GROUND
WATER TANK
WATER COL
WHEEL DROP
ENGINE SHED
UP (DONOHUE) SIDINGS
DOWN (TOP) SIDINGS
FAIRFIELD STATION
From Stockport

The 10.45 Higher Buxton "shunt" passes over Spring Gardens viaduct on a typically snowy day in the winter of 1964-65. In the background, the now roofless Midland Station can be seen. After shunting at Higher Buxton, this locomotive will spend the rest of the day shunting and banking trains as required, as well as working the "cross-roaders", the name given to the transfer freights from the Down to the Up sidings.   *J.M.Bentley*

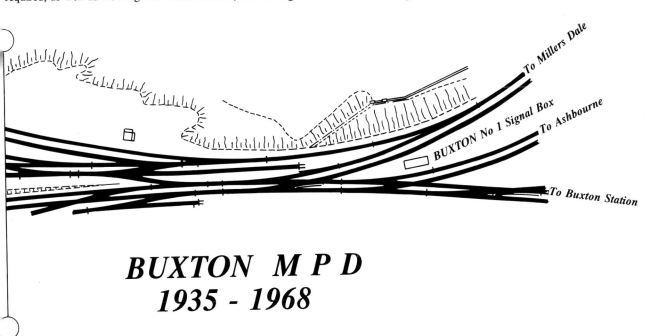

BUXTON M P D
1935 - 1968

LNWR Buxton. New Depot. c.1898. It was in August 1891 that a report was submitted to the LNWR management to the effect that a new locomotive shed was urgently required at Buxton. At this time the old depot had to cope with nine locomotives, only four of which could be got under cover in the existing shed. Accomodation for at least twelve engines was requested, and more than adequately met by the provision of the typical LNWR 'North Light' type structure illustrated. This covered six roads, five of them 195 feet in length and one 180 feet long, with a total capacity to house 24 locomotives, but the only locomotive in view in this photograph is a Webb 17 inch 'Coal engine'. This is probably the right time to look at the depot's work, and at some of the destinations to which the men worked. During the late 1880s the importance of lime, and limestone grew considerably, thus, with the opening of the line to Hindlow and Harpur Hill, followed quite quickly by the direct line to Parsley Hay, considerable alterations took place. A great deal of the tonnage off the Hindlow line went towards the Liverpool area; Clock Face, St Helens, features prominently in the workings, the fast expanding glass producing industry in that area drawing in a big supply of the best quality limestone. Garston, Edge Hill, and Widnes were three other regular destinations, as was Oldham. At all these locations Buxton men lodged for many years. More local work took them to Macclesfield, Edgeley, and Longsight, as well as the High Peak section; men were moved into the new depot from Longsight, Edgeley and other LNWR depots, all given just the customary 48 hours notice of the transfer.   *Authors Collection*

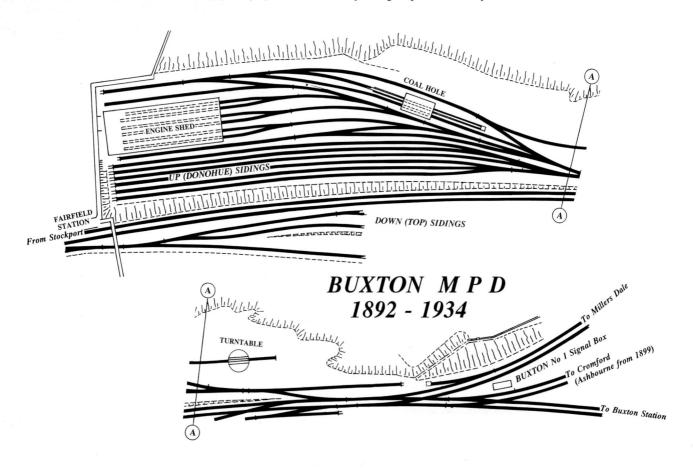

BUXTON M P D
1892 - 1934

Buxton LNWR Depot. c.1898.
Just two of the old Allan 'Crewe Goods' locomotives were fitted with cabs, one of these being No.**3022**. This fascinating veteran started life as a 2-4-0 tender locomotive, No.**307** 'Fury', built in March 1853; she was rebuilt as a tank locomotive in January 1867, became duplicate list No.1879 in July 1883, and was renumbered in the new duplicate list as No.3022 in January 1888. She survived at Buxton until withdrawn in June 1904, and her last days were spent working with the contractors building the Ashbourne line, and after its completion she was used as the coal bank engine, and spare for C.&.H.P.Rly section duties.
Authors Collection

Buxton. LNWR Depot. c.1896.
Another intriguing Crewe veteran No.**3046** stands on the new depot, just prior to its withdrawal in September 1896; this locomotive started life as No.**332** '*Aberdeen*' in March 1854, then carried the No.**1891**, in 1880 and, finally was No.**3046** in January 1888.
Authors Collection

Buxton. LNWR Depot. c.1896.
An interesting visitor was this 0-4-0 saddle tank, No.**3243**, which was probably used as a coal bank locomotive, or had been on loan to one of the local quarry concerns, no records exist of it being used on the C.&.H.P.Rly section. In latter days locomotives of this class were loaned to the Grin Quarry when their own engine was away for repair. The original design for this machine was produced under the superintendance of John Ramsbottom, but this particular machine was built during F.W.Webb's regime at Crewe in November 1892, so despites its aged appearance was only relatively new when the picture was taken.
Authors Collection

Heaton Chapel. 1880s. This interesting photograph shows a Buxton DX Goods engine No. **1565** on a stopping train to Manchester, London Road, a picture very likely taken by Mr P.F.Cooke who, during this period took many outstandingly good photographs, both at this location and also at London Road station. The train was no doubt equipped with two brake vans, one next to the locomotive and the other at the rear, skilful co-operation was required between the driver and the two brakesmen to stop the trains at some of the heavily graded stations on 'our' line. The following incident was reported in the 'High Peak News' of the 8th July 1882. *"On Saturday evening last a singular occurrence took place to a train leaving Buxton for Manchester at 8.50 pm. After leaving Dove Holes the brakes of the locomotive broke, and when trying to stop for Chapel-en-le-Frith the Driver could not do so and ran on to Whaley Bridge, where it was brought to a halt. The passengers for Chapel-en-le-Frith were conveyed forward in a special train."* So! travel could be quite a precarious business in the days before the continuous brake.

Authors Collection

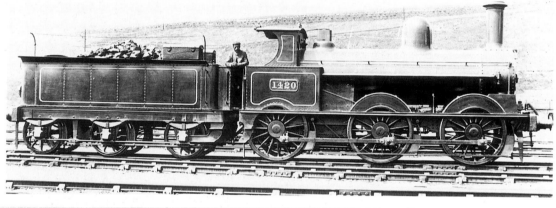

Buxton. LNWR Depot. c.1894. The long serving Ramsbottom DX Goods engines were, in many instances, rebuilt by F.W.Webb and fitted with larger boilers and vacuum brakes, but still only actuating twelve wooden brake blocks. Here we see Buxton Depot's No. **1420**, standing in front of Brown Edge before any houses were built on the land in the rear. This locomotive was, then, fresh out of Crewe works following her rebuild in January 1894, she was originally built in May 1865 and not scrapped until May 1922. *Authors Collection*

Buxton. LNWR Depot. c.1900. Another view of a Buxton 'Special DX Goods',(as the rebuilt engines were known), as No.**1594** awaits her turn under the coal hole.

Authors Collection

Buxton LNWR. Depot. c.1900. A Webb 17 inch Coal engine stands on the ash pit road of the new depot, a spot where many photographs were taken. Driver Chappell stands on the footplate, this man, like many of the older drivers at Buxton had spent many years on the Cromford and High Peak sections. The locomotive No.**2448**, built in July 1882 was transferred, along with many others to the R.O.D. in 1917 and was sent abroad, not to return.   *Courtesy E.Plant*

Buxton. LNWR. Depot. c.1896. Another Webb 17 inch 0-6-0 stands especially for the photographer, complete with its cleaners, and again, Driver Chappell; No.**146** had not, at this time, been fitted with brakes on the locomotive.

Authors Collection

Whaley Bridge. February 1885. A very unfortunate accident befell one of Buxton's 17 inch 0-6-0 Coal engines on the night of Tuesday, 17th February 1885. The locomotive concerned had been down in Shallcross Siding carrying out shunting duties and, after completion, was returning towards Whaley Bridge, the signal for which was showing clear but, unfortunately, it was frozen in the clear position, whilst the trap points lay for the stop block, situated adjacent to the bridge, opposite to what is now Plants Furnishing Store. The crew, huddled together on the footplate for protection from the elements were totally unaware of the impending disaster. The engine hit the stop block and plunged down into the roadway, killing the Driver, Robert Bagshaw and the Guard, William Moores; the fireman James Morten, sustained rib injuries, but survived. The picture shows the back-breaking task of retrieving the locomotive and tender a few days later, using only 10 ton hand-cranes to complete the dangerous and arduous task. *Authors Collection*

Buxton. LNWR Depot. c.1900 On pages 26 and 27 there are illustrations showing a major incident on the old turntable, prior to which a "practice run" had been made by a Webb 17″ Coal Engine No **2276**. The driver, T.Wilshaw, was somewhat luckier than his counterpart on 1635, whose tank locomotive had come to grief in great style. As can be seen here, **2276** buried itself into the masonry of the table hole and was counter balanced by its tender. Even so, its retrieval proved difficult with there being no jacking space at the front of the locomotive and with the turntable being half way round, other locomtives could not be attached to the rear to "snatch" 2276 back to safety.

Buxton. LNWR. Depot. c.1900. The next class of goods engine to come to Buxton, after the DX goods and the Coal engines, was the 18 inch goods, or 'Cauliflowers' as they were universally known, because they carried the company crest on the driving splashers which, when viewed from a distance certainly looked like the aforementioned vegetable. They were in fact, a very fine locomotive, this example No.**59**, was built in November 1899 and is seen here, as new, on the ashpit. These locomotives were used as much on passenger as on goods turns, in fact the crews preferred them on passenger workings on account of the fact that eighteen full turns of the reversing wheel were needed to move from full foward to full back gear, making shunting operations rather a strenuous job. No.59 had a relatively short life however, she was allocated LMS No.8504, but never carried it, being broken up as No.59 in September 1928.

Authors Collection

Buxton Shed. Cleaners. c.1898. Foreman cleaner Oldfield (second from left on the back row), and the cleaning staff appear in this picture, although only a few can be identified. To the left of Mr Oldfield are T.Swann, J.Sharpe, and W.Hawley; far right, on the front row is G.Boulton. After taking this picture the unknown, but accomplished photographer took a shot of the whole engine, a Webb 5 ft 6 inch 2-4-2 tank, No.**2132**, with just three men posing for the camera.
Authors Collection

Buxton. LNWR. Depot. c.1895. The very capable Webb 5 ft 6 inch 2-4-2 tanks arrived in the mid 1890s, replacing the compound tank locomotives on the London Road services, plus working the short lived express' to Liverpool, Lime Street via Davenport Junction and Cheadle Village Junction; they also took part in the Macclesfield services. The upper picture shows No.**427**, well coaled up with large lumps which will, by the time they have been broken to size, enable the fireman to shovel them through the one foot square coal hole in the cab back plate having, meantime, caused him a great of heavy work. *Authors Collection*

Manchester, London Road. c.1895. The first locomotive of this class, No.**910**, is here seen on the turntable at Manchester, London Road, with Driver Robert Gartside leaning on the footframe. In typical LNWR style the fireman holds the long oil feeder in readiness to 'spot round'. The fireman always carried out this duty on the LNWR, whereas on the Midland Railway the fireman would never be allowed to oil round, that was for the driver only to do, a precept that was strictly adhered to. *Authors Collection*

Buxton Shed. c.1898. Webb 5 ft 6 inch 2-4-2 tank, No.**2132**
Authors Collection

Buxton LNWR. Depot. c.1920. The Webb 2-4-0T's (known as Chopper tanks) were a part of the depot's locomotive comple-ment for over 60 years, so two pages of pictures of them on, or around the depot are surely justified. The first two are of No.**1443** in, and around the 'coal hole', on the first Driver William Holgate and Fire-dropper Clayton are in the cab, whereas the second picture of No.**1443** shows her after moving along towards the ash pit, with another member of the class above and alongside, up on the coal bank, ready to take away empty wagons and replace them with full. This locomotive, along with four others has an interesting history. When Webb first introduced this class of 2-4-0 tank engines in 1876, 50 in all, they proved to be excellent machines but, the tiny coal bunker restricted their use so, in the late 1890s they were replaced by the 2-4-2 tanks, which took the same numbers as their predecessors, excepting for ten which were retained in their 2-4-0T form for use on the Cromford & High Peak section. It was found, by 1905, that more 2-4-0 tank engines were needed so five of the 2-4-2 tanks were then cut down down and transformed into 2-4-0's, in a complete reversal of the first re-building. No.**1443** was one of the engines so treated; in this form they were used on motor train work for a few years, but all gradually found their way to Buxton, although a couple were kept at Longsight to work E.C.S.duties and as spare engines, the remainder were spread around from Buxton to Cromford. The two lower pictures, taken at the bottom of the coal tank show Nos.**2238** and **2240**, plus Drivers W.Goodwin and C.Bagshaw.
Authors Collection

Buxton. LNWR. Depot. c.1920. Chopper Tank No.**1443** with Driver William Holgate and Fire-dropper Clayton.   *Authors Collection*

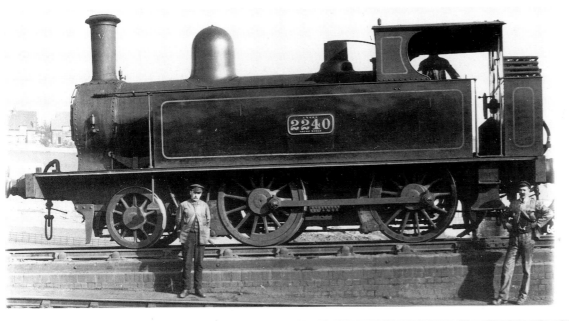

Buxton. c.1920. 2-4-0T No.**2240** at the bottom of the coal bank with Driver C.Bagshaw.
Authors Collection.

Buxton. LNWR. Depot. c.1920. Chopper tank No.**2243** is busy about coal bank duties in the typical winter conditions prevailing in the Buxton area at this period.
Authors Collection

Buxton. LNWR. Shed. c.1920.
2-4-0T No.**2248** is, on this occasion seen in the depot, in the left background is a Midland Railway five-plank open wagon, and building development has commenced, with houses appearing below the rise on Brown Edge.
Authors Collection

Buxton. Depot. LNWR. c.1920
No.**2280** has halted, momentarily, in its task of shunting ash wagons whilst this photograph has been taken, Driver Jack Heath is on the footplate.   *Authors Collection*

Buxton. 1920s. Similarly to former No.2240, 2-4-0 tank No.**2244** got to carry a new LMS number, **6424** in her case, but it will be noticed that No.6424, unlike No.6422 in the preceding picture has also attained to the dignity of having a new number-plate also displayed on the smokebox door. *Authors Collection*

Buxton LNW. c.1901. For much of the local freight work to Briggs, Parsley Hay, Harpur Hill and such like, the Webb 17" 'Coal' tanks, or "Bashers" as they were known were used. This view shows No.**10** standing by the turntable, its bucket hanging in the usual place around the shed label bracket on the cab back spectacle plate. *C. H. Eden.*

Buxton LNW. 1921. No.**158** stands against the well known back-drop of Fairfield Church and the houses in St.Peter's Road and it is interesting to note the steady growth of Fairfield from the photographs contained within this book. The engine has been fitted with cast-iron brake blocks, a situation repeated on other class members over the years. Of the two men on the footplate, only one can be identified and that is Frank Bennett who stands nearest to the left in this view.
Authors collection.

Buxton Up Sidings. c.1900. Webb 17" 0-6-2 tank No.**2361** stands in the Up siding always known to the staff as "Donahue", probably taking its name from the contractor who built it. At the time this photograph was taken the sidings only contained three roads, they were later extended to accommodate seven. The crew stand alongside their highly polished locomotive and although only in plain black, the handrails etc. are shiny metal. To the left the old gentleman in the bowler hat is the same man who was photographed at the controls of the old Crewe Goods 2-4-0 No.**3032** earlier in the book.
Authors collection

Buxton. c.1900. This group of pictures illustrates one of the more dramatic incidents on the new depot, when a practically new Webb 18" 0-6-2 tank No.**1635**, which must have had a regulator valve blowing through badly. Whilst being turned she set off at a considerable rate before plunging over the edge of the turntable and coming to rest with her smokebox pointing to the sky. It took the shed staff a considerable time to bring 1635 back to the rails again. As a result the turntable had to be cut up, the engine being stripped of as many parts as possible before the Longsight breakdown team, plus Buxton fitters, were able, with the use (for the first time) of hydraulic jacks and many sleepers, returned 1635 to an upright position. The magnitude of this task has to be seen to be appreciated. The gentleman in the trilby hat who appears in three of these views was Mr Farmer, the Shed Master, who no doubt had an unpaid holiday awaiting the unfortunate driver involved. At the side of Mr Farmer stands Mr Oldfield, the Foreman Cleaner.
Authors Collection.

Buxton LNW. c.1910. A Webb 6ft 2-4-0 No.795 *Falstaff* awaits departure with the 12/45pm through coach service to London Euston via Ashbourne, Burton-on-Trent and Nuneaton. The driver is Bill Burford, the fireman Jack Pickford. Three of these locomotives were kept at Buxton for this service from about 1902 until its cancellation during the First World War in 1916. At the beginning of this service in October 1899, 18" 0-6-2 tanks were rostered for the job but frequent running out of coal soon saw them replaced by the 18" 0-6-0 "Cauliflowers". After the introduction of the Precursor class engines on the main line expresses, the need for pilot engines decreased and so quite a few of these "Jumbo's", as they were popularly known, became available and were sub-shedded to Buxton from Crewe. The three most regular performers were No.795 *Falstaff*, No.2158 *Sister Dora*, No.231 *Firefly*, with No.763 *Violet* and No.733 *Chimera* also putting in appearances. The spare engine did not stand idle, being rostered to work the Friden goods in a morning, its short wheelbase being ideal for the tight curvature of that line. For the cleaners, passing out as firemen, these were the jobs on which they were sent under the eyes of Drivers Gartside, Burford and Mottram. If a favourable report was received from this trio, they were allowed to fire on passenger trains, a similar test having been carried out previously on goods trains. It was hard luck if your face did not fit. During the duration of these jobs, various fill-in turns were found at Nuneaton, to prevent the men from becoming idle whilst awaiting the slip coach from Euston. Leicester was one place they went to, and the 12/45pm departure from Buxton, after placing their through coach behind an express at Nuneaton, worked to Rugby and back to Nuneaton with a stopping train. The original drivers on this job, Messrs Burford, Gartside and Mottram, had all previously been at Longsight and therefore had route knowledge of Nuneaton and Rugby. *Authors collection.*

Buxton LNW. c.1925. Another Webb 2-4-0 No.**2192** *Caradoc*, blows off furiously whilst awaiting departure with an Engineers observation coach. The engine is standing in for the Engineers own locomotive 'Engineer Manchester'. The signal bell can be seen on the end of the coach. *Authors collection.*

(top and centre). **Buxton LNW Depot. October/November 1907.** To mark the departure for scrap of the last of the old Allan Crewe Goods 2-4-0 tank engines, the company photographer was sent from Crewe to photograph the occasion. This he duly did, having the veteran pose alongside the latest tank locomotive on the depot, a Precursor Tank, No.**111**, built in July 1906, just fifty years to the very month after the old No.**3054**. She had been built in July 1856 as No.**83** and when transferred to the LNW Northern Division, became their No.**483**. Renumbered on the first LNW duplicate list as No.**1930**, her final identity came on the second duplicate list as No.**3054** in October 1889. No.3054 had for many years been on the Cromford & High Peak section, and during a shortage of Webb 2-4-0 'Chopper' tanks, it was decided to fit this one locomotive with the vacuum brake, but not a cab, so it was available to work the vacuum fitted milk traffic from off the C.& H.P. R. section into Buxton. It must have been the only Crewe Goods type ever to have had a vacuum brake and probably accounts for its longevity. However, the Crewe photographer did a good job that day and the scene was well recorded with the shed foreman Mr Needham in the foreground on each picture. *Authors collection.*

Buxton LNW Depot. c.1907. The importance of the Buxton to Manchester passenger service was now being recognised by the LNW. Fierce competition for the lion's share of it was always present, between the Midland and North Western companies, so the same motive power could be found on the very important Watford to Euston services as well as the Manchester suburban services, in fact motive power was regularly exchanged between Watford and Buxton depots. The Precursor tanks were very good locomotives on the Manchester services and came new from Crewe works. They coped well with the loads of the day which were usually up to five of the Webb 42ft radial coaches. Later on, when the very heavy sets of vestibule coaches were introduced, lack of adhesion in bad weather was often their weakness as it had been with the Webb 5' 6" 2-4-2 tanks which had preceded them. Nevertheless, No.**762** makes a fine sight cleaned ready for the next turn of duty. *Authors collection.*

Stockport Edgeley. c.1924. The combined 4/00pm Buxton express and slow train left Manchester London Road double-headed by two Buxton engines. At Stockport the fireman of the leading engine 'hooked off'. This engine then retreating in the "slums", as the centre roads were known, whilst the train engine took the first half of the train express to Buxton, with only a couple of stops. The other locomotive then reattached to the remaining portion and followed to Buxton stopping at all stations. The leading Precursor tank is Buxton's No.**1551**. *E. R. Morten.*

Another spotlessly clean Buxton Precursor tank here with its contingent of cleaners. The cleaning of these locomotives was generally work for six lads, lots being drawn for the various jobs, the best being the boiler, smokebox and cab spectacle plate, the worst the inside motion and wheels, side tanks and bunker being the other job, each emplying two lads. Generally those who were allotted the boiler, finished their work first, and helped out with the wheels and frames to get the job done more quickly. No.**612** was built in March 1907, became LMS No.6812 and was broken up in November 1939.

authors collection.

Buxton LNW Depot. c.1920. Buxton's best Precursor tank, No.**784**, stands on the ashpit line awaiting the firedroppers attention prior to coaling. Drivers W. Goodwin and C. Bagshaw stand alongside the bunker. No.**784** was one of the earlier locomotives of the class with the large diameter bogie wheels, being turned out of Crewe Works in May 1905, the third to be built. She became LMS No.**6782** in May 1927, and was broken up in June 1938, having remained at Buxton until 1927-28, a longer period at the depot than originally intended. The cause of this was the Furness Vale accident involving a bowen Cook Superheater 4-6-2T, a matter that will be dealt with when we come to that class. *Authors collection.*

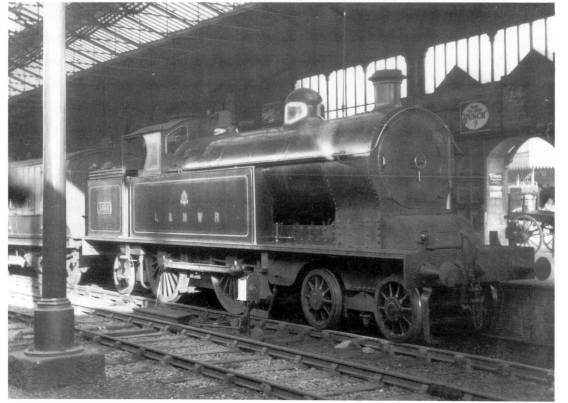

Buxton LNW Station. c.1924. Another Buxton Precursor tank, No.**874** stands on the excursion platform with an evening train to Manchester. There is little to tell from this picture that the LMS had been in existence for over 12 months, both engine and rolling stock being in pure LNW condition. *E. R. Morten.*

Buxton LNW Station. c.1924. One of the 1909 built locomotives, No.**1536**, also a Buxton engine, waits in the main platform after working the 4/00pm train from Manchester. Note the London, suburban destination board brackets on the front framing, an indication that this locomotive has been transferred north, whilst one of the local engines will have been put through Crewe works and then sent south. *E. R Morten.*

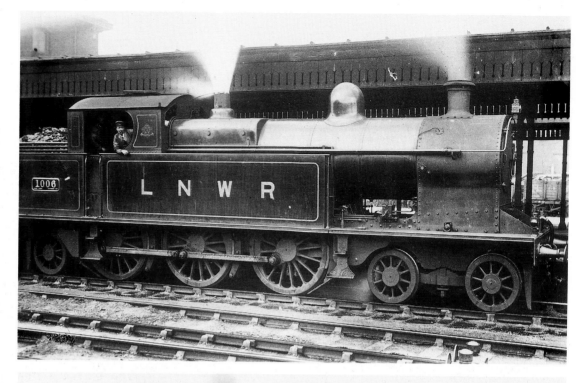

Stockport Edgeley. c.1922. No.1006 was for many years the regular engine of Driver W. Beresford and that gentleman is seen in the cab, posing on the fireman's side. This locomotive became 6974 in 1927, but was transferred away under the block allocation scheme. *Authors collection*

Buxton LNW Station. c. 1924. The largest and by far the most powerful of the LNW passenger tank locomotives to be seen on the service was the Bowen Cooke "Superheater" tanks. These locomotives were designed to cope with the steadily increasing weight and speeds of the suburban and semi-fast trains. Their design went back to F.W. Webb's tank engine wheel size of 5ft 6ins., which with new tyres was 5ft 8½ins. in diameter, with superheated steam and 20" x 26" cylinders, a great increase in power over the older Precursor tanks plus the greatly needed extra adhesion provided by the six coupled driving wheels. It was not until 1920 that the class was allocated to Buxton, some ten years after their first appearance. The Precursor tanks were experiencing difficulty in keeping the faster times expected on the businessmens trains. They had been helped along by the Whale 19" 4-6-0's but basically these were small wheeled goods locomotives and had themselves difficulty in keeping the timings especially down the bank to Stockport. No.841 was probably the first to arrive in late 1920, but others soon followed and as one might expect they soon showed complete mastery of all the services, both fast and slow, but never quite ousting the Precursor tanks. All went well until 5th May 1922, when No.1710 had what could have been a very serious accident, approaching Furness Vale at 6/6pm with the 5/40pm Manchester London Road to Buxton express. Travelling at approximately 55 mph, the left side connecting rod broke through the jack link pin hole with the result that the boiler barrel was pierced by the portion of rod remaining attached to the big end. The hole was situated immediately above the driving axle and was 14" long and 4" wide. Driver Hunter, who was scalded about the legs, was able to bring the train to a stand in some 720 yards from the point where the failure occurred. His fireman was not injured and there was no derailment or damage to the train. This accident worried the authorities very much coming so soon after a similar occurance with a Prince of Wales class locomotive No.877 at Cheadle Hulme on the 28th April that year. Nowadays ultra-sonic testing is available for the identification of hidden cracks etc., but back in 1922, examination was by sight and hammer, with oil or carbide lamps as the only illumination. The Precursor tanks were therefore needed for the faster trains, the 4-6-2 tanks for a time relegated to the slower jobs which completely reversed the reason for allocating them to Buxton. The above picture shows the third member of the class to be built, No.2667, awaiting departure from Buxton with an evening train. To assist the Precursor tanks a Precursor tender engine 4-4-0 No.419 *Monarch* was allocated to Buxton for a while, during 1924-25.

E.R. Morten.

Buxton LNW Station. 1924. A very half-hearted attempt was made by the Crewe authorities in LMS days to renumber their steeds. Just a few were dealt with in 1923 before the whole business was dropped and here we see one of the few which received the treatment. No.**6963** (LNWR No.716) out-shopped from Crewe in December 1923, awaiting departure from the excursion platform with a Manchester slow train. Another interesting fact regarding the renumbering was that the Midland practice of block allocation of numbers to depots commenced in earnest around 1926. Even though the authorities knew what LMS numbers the locomotives should carry, many remained with their old LNWR numbers until 1928. Buxton's block were all supposed to be in the 6990-6996 series, yet 6993 was not renumbered until 1928 and 6995 - ex 2384, in 1927, the latter carrying LMS on its tanks with an LNWR numberplate on the bunker.   *E. R. Morten.*

Chapel-en-le-Frith. 1924. Another early renumbering this time No.**6986** - ex No.1416 - enters Chapel-en-le-Frith with an Up Buxton express, Fireman Tom Murfin on the footplate. The usual five car set is strengthened with two extra coaches. Note the precision signalling, the Up Home signal having been replaced to danger before the third coach has passed!
Authors collection.

Buxton LNW depot. c.1900. After dealing with passenger locomotives it is now the turn of the largest freight locomotives the LNWR possessed. These eight-coupled machines first appeared at the depot in the mid to late 1890's and were many and varied. The first two pictures depict the "parents" of the majority, the 3-cylinder and 4-cylinder compounds turned out by Crewe in great numbers. Here we see a 3-cylinder compound No.1840 standing at the end of the ashpit roads. Whether or not she is a Buxton engine is hard to tell, it is more than likely allocated to Stockport Edgeley. Not many houses are to be seen; Nunsfield Road awaits the builder, but Clifton Bank is visible, one house thereon was used as a lodge for "foreign" train crews for many years.

C. H. Eden.

Buxton LNW station. c.1912. When the freight and tender locomotives became too large for the turntable on the LNW depot, the station witnessed a continual stream of locomotives turning on the triangle before proceeding to the Down sidings for their trains. During such an activity, Buxton depot's 4-cylinder compound No.2024 is pictured here. Known to the staff as "Swammies", these engines were probably the first of the eight-coupled types to be allocated to Buxton. This particular locomotive, No.2024, certainly was. Being built in May 1903 and rebuilt to a 2-cylinder simple G1 class in August 1923, she eventually received LMS No.8934, before once again being rebuilt in December 1945 to class G2a. Withdrawal towards the end of the decade led to her being broken up in March 1950.

W. Beckerlegge.

Buxton Down Sidings November 1921.

The events leading up to the great explosion which took place at 12.45am on the morning of November 11th 1921, have been covered in various articles in the past, but being a happening of great seriousness we will again look at the facts. Engine no.**134**, a Webb 4' 3" 4 cylinder compound 0-8-0 (as 2024 in the previous picture) had been built at Crewe in May 1903, and was still in its original condition, no doubt rebuilding to a 2 cylinder simple was being planned for the future. Crewe Works, like most other railway workshops, had still, in 1921, a vast backlog of repair work resulting from the fact that during the 1914-18 war, locomotive repairs took second place to work with armaments etc. for the war effort. To ease the pressure, Messrs Beardmores undertook to overhaul eighteen eight-coupled goods engines at their Parkhead and Dalmuir works in Glasgow, for at this time that company was engaged in building a batch of new 'Prince of Wales' class 4-6-0's for the LNWR, so a great deal of co-operation was already in existence between Crewe and Glasgow. No.134 was one of the twelve locomotives to go into Parkhead works, and actually spent from October 1920 until July 1921 undergoing repairs. After one or two "light engine" runs, was allocated to Longsight depot on August 4th, but was actually sent to Stockport, which like Buxton, was under the Longsight administration. After resuming revenue earning service it was apparent that No.134 was not the most trouble free of locomotives and was laid off or under repair from August 12th to 23rd. When regular working recommenced, No.134 spent another 10 days out of service from October 28th to November 8th with injector trouble, a regular failing on this class of locomotive but exceptionally bad in the case of No.134. In fact, when one reads the repair reports, one realises that the locomotive was giving far from satisfactory service. On September 23rd Driver Allen of Warrington depot reported what was to be the first sign of impending doom for the locomotive.

He rather quaintly reports: "Steam gauge goes all round", no one realising that all the injector trouble was because the boiler pressure regularly rose above 200 lbs per sq.in. The pressure gauge was reported again on October 22nd, once at Stockport and again at Farnley Junction depot, and finally at Buxton on November 10th by Driver Winstanley of Sutton Oak depot, who had brought the engine up to Buxton and had actually witnessed the gauge reading 300 lbs per sq. in. whilst at Dove Holes. He reported same to Foreman Oldfield at Buxton, but Driver Winstanley actually stated that something more was amiss and 134 would blow up if not sorted out. Nobody really doubted that the safety valves were anything other than ok, yet no one remembers them lifting at all during late October. However, the pressure gauge was once again changed, which meant blowing all the steam out of her. After this, the fire would be re-lit. The locomotive was rostered for the 12.45am Buxton to Oldham freight to which Driver W. Holmes, and Fireman W. Fletcher, after lodging in Fairfield, were to work home to Oldham. Driver G.H. Moss prepared the locomotive, and after preparation, noting the fact that the pressure gauge had been changed, handed No.134 over to Driver Holmes at 11/55pm with 120 lbs per sq.in. boiler pressure. Holmes left the depot at 12.25am, after his fireman had commenced making up the fire. When the Guard, J. Hannah, of Oldham, saw what class of locomotive he had for the train, the load of 40 wagons was reduced by 5. No.134 was used for this job and then backed up onto the train. Giving Driver Holmes the 'right away' signal he started to make his way back towards the brake van. No.134 then started off, making about four exhaust beats before exploding. When one studies the photographs of the position of all the bits of No.134, scattered up to 670 feet away, (these being the large pieces, small ones were found beyond Fairfield churchyard) this was some explosion. A very thorough

(Continued over)

Buxton Down Sidings. November 1921. This and the five photographs on page 36 show the total devastation of No.134, the boiler totally wrecked, the trailing part of the main frame burst open and bent round the trailing driving axle, one wheel plus axle landing in the top of a nearby wagon. The most amazing thing was that the top of the firebox, including safety valve, was flung 540 feet onto the shed, where as luck would have it no one was hit. The picture taken by the late Frank G. Brown shows the firebox wrapper plate and back plate lay in the shed yard, the faulty safety valve casing still in place on top of what was originally a round top boiler. *Authors collection.*

enquiry ensued, alas not much use to the unfortunate crew who were, like the locomotive, in many small pieces. The overhaul at Beardmores was found to have been very carefully supervised by their works foreman and the ever-present LNW works officials, but something had gone amiss, there being slight differences in the clearances between the safety valve webs and the seats plus a difference in the angles of the valve seats themselves, when compared with the locomotives overhauled at Parkhead works and those dealt with at Dalmuir works. The inspectors agreed that too little clearance had been given when cold, so there was little chance of these valves being able to lift off their seats after expansion had taken place. The safety valves off the other seventeen locomotives were hurried to Crewe for testing. No.437 was found to be the same.

No.18 from Bescot depot blew off at 200 lbs. ok.

No.1225 from Abergavenny reached 210 lbs before the lever was lifted to release the valve.

No.1017. this locomotive reached 210 lbs without blowing off

No.647, Crewe South, valve sent into works, would not blow off at all.

The rest blew off between 195 lbs and 205 lbs.

A boiler of similar age was tested at Crewe in the presence of the inspectors and withstood a hydraulic pressure of 600 lbs per sq.in., which shows what magnificent boilers these were.

In summing up, Major Hall, the inspecting officer states: "My general conclusion in this very serious case is that so many factors, some of them not necessarily constituting an element of danger in themselves, contributed to the result that no responsibility can fairly, in the circumstances, be assigned to any individual."

Buxton LNW Station. 25th July 1921. A pair of 0-8-0's destined for the Down sidings await the road out of the main platform during turning on the triangle. The leading engine is a Class G designed by Geo. Whale just before his retirement, and built under Bowen Cooke's regime at Crewe. These locomotives used saturated steam until rebuilt as Class G1 later in their careers. No.**1322** was built in April 1910, rebuilt to G1 class in May 1928. It became LMS No.**9091** in June 1926 and was allocated British Railways No.**49091** but broken up prior to the final renumbering, in September 1949. She is seen here in original condition fitted only with a steam brake, as were all the earlier compound 0-8-0's. This braking system had one great fault - that of being only fitted with one steam cylinder under the footplate and the tender brakes were actuated, as on Webb's locomotives, by a solid bar between engine and tender. This worked well when the gap between engine and tender was normal, but down gradients, just when the brake was badly needed, the weight of the train naturally pushed the tender hard-up to the locomotive, rendering the brake useless. To combat this, all of our locomotives carried a coupling link cut in half, and this 'U' shaped piece of equipment was dropped over the intermediate drawbar (between locomotive and tender) whilst they were working hard towards Bibbingtons summit, this prevented the tender from closing up too much on the descent to Stockport and allowed the brake bar to actuate the tender brakes. No.**1322** was one of the twenty six of the class lent to the R.O.D. in 1917 and sent to France. *National Railway Museum.*

Buxton Down Sidings. 14th November 1921. Whilst the local photographers were busy taking pictures of the remains of No.**134**, a group of firemen employed one to take a picture of them against the new G1 0-8-0 No.**2224**.

Back row on frames: L.to R. No.1. not known; No.2. Jim Murfin; No.3. Bill Heath; No.4. Jack Baker, No.5. Charlie Harrison; No.6. Bill Bowder, No.7. Bill Weston; No.8. Herbert Thornley; No.9. H. Bramwell; No.10, Johnny Green.

Front row: No.1.& No.2. not known; No.3. Albert Bowers; No.4. not known; No.5. Frank Bennett; No.6. not known.

The fireman far left on the front row has his 'double trip' basket on the engine's siderod, most of the lodges the men used provided a bed only, the men bringing their own food to prepare. This man had a wicker basket, others had similar sized metal boxes.

courtesy Mrs K. Bowers.

LNWR 0-8-0's

When the block allocation of loco-motives commenced in the mid 1920's the following batch of 0-8-0's was allocated to Buxton: Nos.**9208-9227,** although the earlier locomotives in the batch were transferred away to Horninglow depot, Burton on Trent. One wonders if the original allocations got a little mixed up between Buxton and Burton, not an unknown occurrence as in latter years the sand dryer meant for Burton was built at Buxton by mistake!

The 0-8-0's arrived as follows:

```
9216 ex Rugby shops 19:02:27
9218 ex Rugby shops 26:02:27
9208 ex Crewe Works 05:03:27
9210 }ex Crewe Works 06:08:27
9219 }
9220 ex Crewe Works 10:09:27
9225 Bescot to Buxton 22:10:27
9209 Edge Hill to Buxton 05:11:27
9224 ex Crewe Works 05:11:27
9217 ex Rugby shops 26:11:27
9213 Springs Branch to Buxton 31:12:27
9211 * see note below 07:01:28
9228 Nuneaton to Buxton 10:03:28
9227 ex Rugby shops 19:05:28
```

Note* No.9211 shown as coming from Rugby and Tebay at the same time!

No.43, later 9215 came from Willesden 07:01:28 and was renumbered at Buxton. As for 9212/14 and 21-23, I have no record of the dates of arrival.

This collection of locomotives were quite a varied lot, some having round top fireboxes, others with Belpaire. Some had steam brake only, others vacuum, and most had Whale "single man's" tenders with just a few having the Bowen Cook "married man's" tender. The four photographs show the different varieties well. The block allocation system soon fell apart, Nos 9208-11 went to Burton Horninglow, with 9210 returning to Buxton some years later. 9227 also disappeared from our allocations leaving 9212 to 9226 to form the basic depot allocation until 1935 when 9217 and 9218 were stranded at Rowsley after that depot ceased to be a sub shed of Buxton. Both were subsequently re-allocated to the Liverpool area. Quite a few of these 0-8-0's were fitted for steam heating, a requirement for the banana trains from Liverpool docks, a job which our engines quiet often found themselves alloted, causing more re-allocations. Even so, quite a few of the original block allocations remained at Buxton until withdrawn, 9210 being the very last. *Authors collection.*

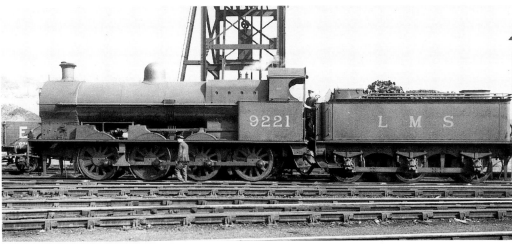

Fairfield Halt. 17th August 1925. Class G1 0-8-0 No.**170** approaches Fairfield Halt with a short goods train. This locomotive was eventually renumbered No.**9255** in June 1926.   *Author's collection.*

Buxton depot. early 1930's. During the early days of the LMS the Webb 2-4-0 tanks were beginning to show signs of old age. To replace them on the C.& H.P. section diagrams came the Webb 0-4-2 "Bissel" tanks, the name coming from the fact that these locomotives were fitted with a solid wheeled bissel truck beneath the cab. They worked alongside the remaining "Chopper" tanks and therefore were to be found on the 'coal bank' duties at Buxton depot. Not being vacuum brake fitted, they did not partake in the milk train duties. One was to be found shunting the Cromford Wharf end of the High peak line, but shown here is No.**7858** with Fireman Tony Newton in the cab, and sister locomotive No.**7859**, both in the shed yard at Buxton.   *Authors collection.*

Buxton Down Sidings. 28th July 1921. Up to the introduction of the 0-8-2 tanks designed by Bowen Cooke in 1911, most of the shunting work at Buxton was carried out by Webb "Chopper" tanks not employed on the C.& H.P. section, and the 17" 0-6-2 tanks (coal tanks). The Down Sidings was a most difficult sidings to shunt as its exit line and shunting neck were on a 1 in 60 gradient, needing a powerful locomotive to be able to lift a heavy train to the stop block under Brown Edge. Having got there, good brakes were required to stop the train pulling the locomotive back to where it had started. Both the Webb designs used were good pullers, but doubtful stoppers. And so, a great improvement was noticed in general ability when four of this class were allocated to Buxton for banking and shunting duties, these being Nos.**482, 1020, 2013** and **2391**. Under the LMS block allocation of 1926, all but **2391** (LMS No.**7899**) were moved away and the new allocation was Nos.**7896/97/98/99**. The picture taken here by the Brown Edge footbridge, shows No.**1090** in very clean condition, as, by now, the war time neglect was beginning to give way to more usual standards of maintenance.
Dr.Cowan/N.R.M.

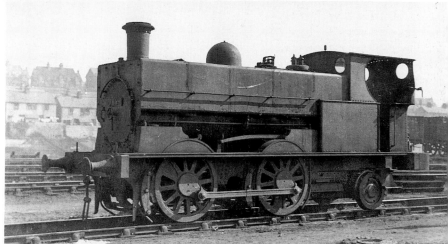

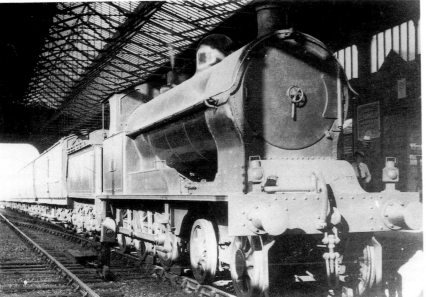

Buxton LNW Station. c.1925. The Whale 19" goods mixed traffic engine No.**1524** awaits the road during turning on the triangle and is coupled to an 0-8-0. These locomotives could be found all over the LNW system on anything from express passenger workings, excursions, coal trains and local pick-up freight. At Buxton they worked passenger turns to Manchester which involved return freight workings, such as the 2.00pm empties from Longsight and the milk empties for the High Peak line. They worked towards Ashbourne and just about every other destination except Friden and Harpur Hill.

The lower picture shows Buxton depot's No.**2614** inside the North Western station having just worked the express portion of the 4.00pm from London Road.   *both photos: E. R. Morten*

Whale 19" goods 4-6-0 No.**1342** awaits departure for Manchester London Road with a slow passenger around the First World War time. This locomotive was one of the later members of the class built in August 1909 .Renumbered 8850 by the LMS in December 1927 and broken up in December 1934.   *courtesy B. Matthews*

The Beames 0-8-4 tanks

These locomotives, like the L.& Y.R. Baltic tanks, first saw the light of day around the last days of their parent company's existence and all were built by the new LMS Company. Early on in LMS days, efforts were made to find locomotives suitable for both freight and passenger turns over the same lines, thus cutting down on the many and varied locomotive classes at each depot. Trials were held using 3F 0-6-0's of Midland design on the passenger services to Manchester London Road, but a derailment at Middlewood cut that short. Prior to that, the then brand new LNW 0-8-4 tanks were tried and were found suitable for freight and all but the fastest passenger turns on the line. Their power was enormous, but with only 4ft 5$^1/_2$ins. diameter driving wheels they threatened to tie themselves in knots whilst working the very fast timed 8.15am and 9.05am expresses to Manchester. Nevertheless No.s**7954** to **7959** were used on all local freight and passenger services, but still the problem of the very fast trains remained. A Precursor 4-4-0 No.**419** *Monarch* was used for a short time, but it was back to the LNWR 4-4-2 and 4-6-2 tanks until the arrival of the Hughes Baltic tanks in 1927.

The top picture shows No.**7956** leaving Manchester with a Buxton express. No.**7955** awaits departure from Chapel-en-le-Frith with the Up empty stock train, coaches, vans and milk vans etc. All were transferred away from Buxton to South Wales and Edge Hill, Liverpool, and the type did not reappear until the 0-8-2 tanks were being withdrawn during and after the last war, their final duties being banking, shunting and snowploughs. The other pictures shows them very much at the end of their days, the last being scrapped in 1949, their duties then performed by the double cabbed LNW 0-8-0's.

Authors collection.

Buxton LNW. 1928. After the grouping of the railway companies in 1923, it soon became apparent that a variety of locomotives might be suitable for lines not on the parent system. The large tank engines owned by the old Furness, Lancashire & Yorkshire, and London, Tilbury & Southend systems were moved around to see if they were of greater use on other lines. The suburban services within the Manchester South area were still in the hands of the LNWR types and after the experiment with the Beames 0-8-4 tanks nothing much was done until 1926 when one of the Furness Railway Baltic tanks, No.**11100** arrived at Longsight for trials in and around Manchester. No photographs or records seem to exist regarding the suitability of this locomotive, for it soon returned to its own system. The next type tried only lived just around the corner, being the newly built LMS/Hughes 4-6-4 tanks used on the Central section lines from Manchester Victoria. On October 29th 1927, Nos.**11110** and **11111** replaced two LNW 4-6-2 tanks Nos.**6968** and **6969** at Buxton and were found suitable for working the services to Manchester London Road. They were joined by No.**11113**, ex Horwich Works, on February 18th 1928 and Nos.**11112** and **11114** from Longsight on March 24th 1928. At this time the class of ten locomotives was shared equally between Longsight and Buxton, Nos. 11115-9 being at the former depot. A great number of exchanges took place, 11112 and 11114 being sent back to Longsight on 21st April 1928 and replaced by two LNWR 4-6-2 tanks Nos.**6977** and **6978** from Stockport. For one short period no less than eight of the Baltics were at Buxton. Very imposing locomotives they were, but how the crews detested them, four sets of valve gear to oil, L.& Y.R. lifting injectors, always in need of a bucket of cold water to cool them down, and worst of all, after being used to the large cab spectacles on LNW 4-4-2 and 4-6-2 tanks, so that good forward vision could be obtained **without** putting ones head out. These locomotives had little forward vision through the small cab front spectacles. This, with their enormous width, drivers had to choose very carefully when to put their heads out. The two views show clearly how they towered above the old LNW stock. They were very capable machines and had no difficulty whatsoever in keeping time on all the services from Buxton. It is fair to say that they were much more up to date than the older LNWR types replaced, but were much more suited to working Blackpool and Southport expresses from Manchester than the London Road suburban services.   *(both photos:) E. R. Morten.*

Buxton. Former LNWR MPD. c.1934. Against the familiar backdrop of Nunsfield Road, the new passenger motive power can be seen; three Fowler 2-6-4 tanks and a Hughes-Fowler 2-6-0 are in , and around, the old coaling stage whilst, in the foreground a 'D' tank awaits its next task in the down sidings.   *H.Townley*

Uttoxeter. c.1932. Driver Joe Norton and Fireman Jack Baker, in cheerful mood beside Buxton's Fowler 2-6-4T No.2370. Sadly, just a while after this picture was taken a tragedy took place when, whilst going to the signal box at Disley LNW, Fireman Baker was struck and killed by a passenger train. *Dr J.Hollick*

Uttoxeter. c.1932 Buxton Fowler 2-6-4T No.2369 with Driver Tommy Swann and Fireman Fred Hough posing for their photograph on the front end.
Dr J.Hollick

Buxton. c.1949-50. Almost two decades after the Uttoxeter pictures were taken, and after nationalisation, 2-6-4T No.42366 still carries the LMS legend on its side-tanks; the Fowler tank is leaving the depot prior to a London Road passenger turn, Fireman John Featherstone, who at this time fired for Driver Jim Thorpe, is peering out of the cab. *N.K.Harrop*

Buxton. Former LNWR Depot. c.1932. Two views of a scene soon to be totally altered by the enlargement, and modernisation of the depot. The amalgamation of motive power can be observed here, with the MR 4F 0-6-0 No.**3842** being coaled up, but the 'spare' High Peak engine is still a 'Chopper Tank'. These covered 'coal holes' were terrible places in which to work, any emission of smoke from the engines brought about terrible rebukes from the men who worked there, upon the heads of the offending driver and fireman.

Authors Collection.

Buxton LNW Depot 1934. The old Webb 2-4-0T still on coal bank duties is surrounded by the then latest passenger motive power the Fowler 2-6-4 tank No.**2332** in the foreground. The work of enlarging the depot has begun, a new water column lays on the ground awaiting erection. *photo: W. Potter courtesy Brian Arnold*

Buxton. LNWR Depot enlargement c.1934-5. During the period that the depot was being enlarged Harry Townley lived in Brown Edge and was, therefore, in just the right place to record the gradual changes especially the construction of the massive concrete coaling plant, which became a feature of the landscape for over 30 years and made the job of coaling up tenders quicker and less labour intensive. The tipping work required in connection with the building of the extension was not without its mishaps and, in the first picture we see that a rake of wagons have gone down the tip, instead of just the spoil loaded into them; needless to say no attempt was made to recover the errant vehicles. The work on the coaling plant was underway early in the winter of 1934/5, its progress can just be observed behind the exaust from No.**9223**'s chimney, as she leaves the Down sidings with freight. By the time the better weather arrived the tower was getting quite large, and by the arrival of summer the top was on. It can be seen in the last two pictures that the raised coal bank has finally been removed, which must have made coaling up very difficult whilst the alterations were in progress. An ex North London tank, at this time the Cromford and High Peak section motive power carries out the duties formerly done by Webb's 'Chopper' tanks, namely the shunting of Loco Coal wagons; the old 'D' tank in the right foreground does not seem to have moved very far whilst all these pictures were being taken. *All Five Photos H. Townley.*

Buxton MPD. Date ?? One of the depot's ex Midland 2P 4-4-0s No.461, which were still in charge of most of the passenger trains on the Midland lines, is posed with Driver Goodwin in front of the buffer, Driver Harold Sigley on the far right and Fireman Frank Martin standing by the smokebox.
Courtesy F.Martin

Buxton MPD. c.1936. 0-8-2 tank No.7898, formerly No.2348 in LNWR days, stands under the new coaling tower. No.7898 carries its new shed plate, with the distinctive white enamel background. This locomotive, part of the block allocation of four, served at Buxton until withdrawal in January 1946; the driver is George Boulton and the Fireman Johnny Green.
Authors Collection

Buxton MPD. Date-late 1930'. In view of all the trouble experienced by the LNWR from having its turntable perched high on an embankment, one would have thought that the last mistake that the LMS authorities would make would be to locate their new turntable in just such a place. The well known inability of former LNWR engines to stand still was also, again, underestimated and 0-8-0 No.9315 made a name for itself by setting back long before the proper time, and attempting to empty its tender down the embankment. Luckily for all, the tender buried itself in the soft earth and this prevented the whole lot descending into the sewerage depot plant below. *E.R.Morten*

Buxton MPD. Saturday, 26th September 1942. Probably the most unusual locomotive ever to visit an ex LNWR depot in this part of the world was this 'Stirling' South Eastern Railway Class F1 4-4-0, a type known on their own system as 'Flying Bedsteads'. Originally built in 1891, and later rebuilt with a larger boiler these locomotives spent many years at the head of the Continental boat trains out of London Victoria, but by the time this photograph was taken, old age and a World War had made No.**1060** redundant on her own system. Along with some of her sister locomotives No.**1060** was loaned to the LMS railway to perform light duties around Derby and Burton-on-Trent, thus releasing more powerful locomotives for tasks of greater importance. In this picture No.**1060** is seen awaiting coal and water before returning to the Midland station to re-couple to the Derby Divisional Superintendent's saloon; this gentleman, Colonel Rudgard obviously felt that, even with a war on, he was entitled to have trips around the system.
H.Townley

Buxton MPD. c.1943. Another newcomer to the Cromford & High Peak section was this Kitson built 0-4-0 saddle tank, seen here on No.13 road; it has probably come to Buxton for a 'hot' axle box to be attended to. After 1935 the responsibility for the C.&.H.P.Rly section locomotives was handed over to Rowsley, a sensible enough decision in regard to those engines working on the southern end of the line, but ridiculous in the case of those stationed at Hopton and Middleton Top, as they had to pass Buxton depot on their way to Rowsley. Driver Frank Martin and John Morten are posing with No.**7000**. *E.R.Morten*

Buxton MPD. 1946/7. After Hitler's War ended the Stanier 2-8-0s began to visit the area more frequently, and were to be found on turns previously worked by the LNWR 0-8-0s. No.**8134** stands on the turntable, with Driver Eric Wilson leaning from the cab window, and John Morten and another driver standing by the tender. *E.R.Morten*

Following the cessation of the last war, the Stanier 8F's and Riddles 'Austerity' locomotives began to return from overseas duties in great numbers and, as with the R.O.D. (Great Central 2-8-0's) after World War I, work had to be found for them. The consequence was massive withdrawals of older types of freight engines all over the country, and this example of a typical War Dept. 2-8-0 having just 'banked' a train from Stockport, awaits its turn on the ash pit, where both fire, and ash pan, will be cleaned. Still carrying its W.D.number in the 71000 series, air and vacuum braked and also fitted, front and back for steam heating passenger stock, these locomotives were regularly seen all over the railway system, until their withdrawal in the mid 1960's.
E.R.Morten

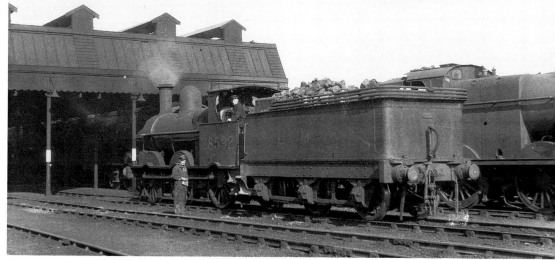

Buxton MPD. c.1947. This must have been the very last visit of a Webb 18 inch 0-6-0 to the area, the 'Cauliflowers,' like the Webb 17 inch Coal engines had been gone from the Buxton scene for many years when this picture was taken. Carrying her final No.**28592**, originally LNWR No.559 built in March 1901, renumbered LMS 8592 in December 1926, placed on the duplicate list as 28592 in 1944, she was finally broken up at Crewe in March 1950.
E.R.Morten

Buxton MPD. 1949. The last LNWR Claughton 4-6-0 No.**6004**, did its final few weeks work on the Buxton to Manchester service, not bad, since the class was officially banned from the Buxton branch because of clearance problems in the Disley and Eaves tunnels. This engine, like the rest of the last survivors of the class, was not in the original LNWR condition; they were reboilered in early LMS days, in an attempt to improve their steaming abilities, this representative of the class was originally named *Princess Louise* a name surrendered to a newer Stanier Pacific in the mid 1930s. No.6004, along with the other remaining LNWR passenger locomotives, was, regretably broken up at Cewe later that year.   *E.R.Morten*

Buxton No.1. Date unknown. A wintry view from No.1 Junction signal box, shows a platelayer awaiting the signalman's instructions as to which points to clean, and clip, for the next move of the two snow-plough engines. This sort of weather meant miserable conditions for all railwaymen, but none more so than the platelayer's who had their work cut out to keep even the minimum amount of point and signal movement free and, judging by the amount of snow on the front of the plough engine, one or two really substantial drifts have been encountered and demolished.
Authors Collection

Buxton MPD. 1947. Foreman Joe Wilson stands in front of the 0-8-0 tank No.7954 after its rescue from Briggs Sidings, after being snowed in (despite the fact that it was fitted with a snow-plough), and abandoned by its crew; it literally took weeks to thaw these locomotives out. No.7954 was withdrawn in December 1948.
E.R.Morten

Buxton Up Sidings. Date unknown. One of the worst problems arising from a bad snowfall was the disposal of the snow removed when cleaning out points, rodding, and walkways in the sidings, heaps got larger and larger, the problem heightened every time there was another fall, and finally it would be necessary to load the snow into wagons so that it could be taken away and dumped or, perhaps just allowed to melt in the wagons. In this view it can be seen that the Up Sidings is being got ready for a snow removal session. *E.R.Morten*

Buxton MPD. 1947. Two more views of the frozen up No.7954 follow, and in this, the first, a cab view shows just how the driven snow had penetrated and what a state the locomotive was in, even the old gauge lamps are frozen into its position at the side of the right-hand water gauge glass; note the extension to the regulator handle to give the driver greater ease of handling, whilst engaged in shunting work. Imagine, too the conditions endured by the men working on these comparatively open footplates, in blizzard conditions, before their locomotives finally became stuck in the snow drifts.   *E.R.Morten*

(left). **Buxton MPD. 1947.** In the second of the photographs, Fitters Frank Brown, Jim Lomas and Shedman Fred Oldfield pose in front of the slowly thawing **No.7954.**   *The late Frank Brown*

Buxton MPD. 1947. LMS 4F No.**4382** was also rescued from the 14 ft deep drifts at Briggs Siding, and thaws out, alongside No.7954; so many ploughs had been broken during clearance operations in this severe winter, that the ridulously small one fitted to No.4382 represents the only one that was left for her final efforts, although her companion in the rear carries the larger version. *E.R.Morten*

Buxton Depot. 1948/9. After the disastrous winter of 1947, it was quite obvious that better snow ploughs were needed, and three new all steel types were introduced; the largest were fitted to the LMS 4F 0-6-0s, whose tenders were given a top shutter to keep snow out of the coal, and side plates fitting between engine and tender protect the crew, whilst the cab sides were equipped with small protectors which contained two windows. In this photograph No.**4339** is fitted up ready for snow clearance duties, whilst in front of, and just to the left of the small booster cabin lies a smaller wooden plough of the older type ready for fitting to No.**9210**, the other plough engine. Ploughs similar to the two smaller of the all steel type were used extensively in Scotland on 5MT 4-6-0s. When necessary the power of the two plough engines was enhanced by putting either 0-8-0s or 2-8-0s between Nos.**4339** and **9210**; Driver Bert Price and Fireman John Plant are seen with No.**4339**. *E.R.Morten*

Buxton Depot. c.1948 Driver Joe Kirk is featured on his LMS 5XP 4-6-0 No.**5568** *Western Australia*, no doubt after working the 5.22 pm from Manchester Central. *Courtesy Jim Kirk*

Buxton MPD. Undated. Driver Teddy Dawson stands in front of 3F 0-6-0 No.**43278**, long associated with Buxton depots, Driver Dawson was tragically killed at Wraggs Brickworks sidings, between Parsley Hay and Hartington, when he fell between the engine and tender of an LNWR 0-8-0. *J.J.Wooliscroft*

Romiley. Sunday, 22nd October 1950. Regular visits were made over the years to Davies & Metcalfe's works at Romiley, the firm's name being synonymous with precision engineering and locomotive injectors. Here, on a visit to look round the works and examine various models of injectors are members of the locomen's M.I.C, (Mutual Improvement Class) together with some members of the Buxton Model Engineering Society.

(1)Bus Driver (2)Insp.Woodruffe (3)Harry Rhodes (4) Unknown (5)Walter Dixon-BMES (6) Phil Murray -BMES (7)Alf Kitchen (8)Sam Whibberley (9)John Wooliscroft (10)Jack Brookes (11) A V Simpson (12) Brian Palfreyman (13)Bill Bennett (14)Wood Jnr (15)Charlie Robinson (16)Eric Needham (17)non railway (18) Fred Bretherton (19)Jack Wood (20)Simpson Jnr (21)Ray Sherwood (22)Herbert Mather (23)Joe Kirk (24) Peter Bretherton (25)Frank Bagshaw (26)Sid Brotherton (27)Geo Fisher (28)Keith Bagshaw (29)Bill Lewis (30)Jim Gilman (31)Frank Wilson (32)Rolley Fidler (33)Derek Wain (34)Frank Palfreyman (35)Bill Gyte (36)Harry Townley

Buxton MPD. Sunday, 24th June 1951. Probably the very first visit of any B.R. standard locomotive to Buxton was this occasion; a brand new 5MT 4-6-0 No.**73005** stands on the depot with Driver Bill Moody alongside.   *E.R.Morten*

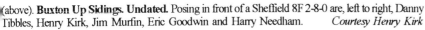

(above). **Buxton Up Sidings. Undated.** Posing in front of a Sheffield 8F 2-8-0 are, left to right, Danny Tibbles, Henry Kirk, Jim Murfin, Eric Goodwin and Harry Needham. *Courtesy Henry Kirk*

(above - right). **Hindlow. c.1951.** 3F 0-6-0 No.**43278** is again featured, with Driver George Fisher, Fireman Wilf Cox and Guard George Sherwin. *Courtesy Martin Fisher*

(below-left). **Buxton Midland station. c.1958.** Driver Herbert Thornley and his Fireman Terry Corrigan were in charge of 2P No.**41905** on this occasion. *J.M.Bentley*

(below-right). **Buxton. Midland Station. Undated.** This is the first of four pictures showing regular 'pull and push' crews; Fireman John Featherstone, Driver George Rickman and Driver Bob Heathcote are featured with No.**58083**, the last of the old MR 0-4-4 tanks used on this service, the engine was withdrawn in 1957. *Courtesy J.Featherstone*

Buxton Midland Station. Undated. The 'push and pull' crews standing before the camera in the station forecourt are : Drivers Walter Palfryman and Bob Heathcote, together with Firemen Bob Bailey and Harold Brown.

Courtesy B Palfryman

Buxton Midland station. 1954. This picture was taken in June 1954, when Driver Frank Boulton was on his last few days before retirement, with him are his regular fireman, Frank Mellor and Guard Jack Brookes. *Courtesy Mrs. R. Baldwin.*

Buxton Depot. Fitting Staff. 1930's. When one is compiling a book of this type, locomen generally get more of the limelight than do the shed staff, doubtless because of the greater number of footplate men. At Buxton, especially following the amalgamation of the two depots, there was a large contingent of fitters, boiler-smiths, tubers, and all manner of shed personnel who were essential to the running of the depot. The first two pictures, taken between a pair of Midland Railway 4-4-0 driving wheels, show some of the older members of the staff and come from the photo album of the late Frank Brown. This, group of four, comprises Fitters Depledge, Brown and Latham, and an unknown fourth member of the staff. *Album the late Frank Brown*

Buxton MPD. 1930's. Of this larger group of men, again posed between the pair of 4-4-0 driving wheels, only Frank Brown, top left, and Fitter Depledge, next to him in the back row can be identified. Some of these men will be working on the new, water pressure powered wheel drop, which made attending to the re-metalling of axle boxes much easier, and certainly quicker than when using the old shear-legs, which required much more man-handling and physical effort. *Album the late Frank Brown*

Buxton MPD. 1960's. The driving wheels of 4F No.**44339** stand outside the fitting shop, awaiting the replacement of the axle boxes following re-metalling, the picture clearly shows the arrangement of big-ends and forward and reverse eccentrics. As well as maintaining 'our own' allocation of locomotives, the fitters had a great deal of work to do on other depot's locomotives. Fowler and Stanier tanks came for mileage attention from Heaton Mersey and Stockport depots, even Trafford Park sent us ex Great Central Railway Director Class 4-4-0s, to be seen to on on our wheel drop. On one occasion when Royal Scot 4-6-0 No.**46111** ran hot at Millers Dale on a St Pancras to Manchester express, our fitters were sent out to deal with it, and whilst working on the engine, having got it back to Buxton depot, whilst the left side motion was being dismantled, to everyone's horror and dismay, the left-side driving wheel fell off, due to the effects of the over-heating the axle had broken behind the wheel end, and only the motion parts were holding it on, fortunately no one was close enough to be hit by the falling wheel. The engine then had to wait for a new pair of 6 ft 9 inch drivers to come from Crewe works before the whole locomotive could be despatched to Crewe for heavy works attention. *Authors Collection*

Buxton MPD. Mid 1950s. The fitters in this group photograph, also from Sid Milner's collection, shows Left to Right : back row, F Barnett, Unknown, Stan Champion, Joe Pocock, Harry Maddocks and Brian Middleton, and L.to R: front row, Alf Boam, Sid Milner and Peter Dempsey. *Sid Milner's Album*

Buxton MPD. 1950s. In addition to the wheel drop, the newly enlarged LNWR depot was given a new fitting shop, complete with an axle box turning lathe, and in this photograph Fitter Sid Milner is depicted dealing with an axle box. *Sid Milner's Album*

Buxton MPD. late 1950s. This is Buxton as most who knew it, remember it, with almost 45 engines spread between the 13 roads, and the drop pit (not numbered). The usual motive power ranged from Midland 3F 0-6-0s to Stanier 8F 2-8-0s, for freight work, and the Fowler 2-6-4 tanks to perform the passenger duties; by the time this picture was taken, however, most of the 2-6-4 tanks had been transferred away, because of the arrival of the D.M.U.s for the services to Manchester, London Road. *N.K.Harrop*

Buxton MPD. 30th March 1957. Two fitters hold over the spring points giving access to the drop pit, as the battered remains of No.**48188** are slowly propelled forward. This was the locomotive involved in the dreadful crash at Chapel-en-le-Frith the previous month, in which Driver John Axon and Guard Creamer of Stockport were killed. The tender attached to the 2-8-0 was sent from Derby works to be coupled to No.**48188**, as its own was so badly damaged as to be unsafe.
E.R.Morten

Buxton MPD. 30th March 1957. Buxton's 4F No.**44339** with an ol Midland tender as a barrier vehicle, places No.**48188**'s tender on th turntable, in readiness for turning, before both the engine and tende involved in the Chapel-en-le-Frith accident started on their slow journey t Derby works for repairs. Driver Harry Mellor is in No.**44339**'s cab, whils Drivers Bert Smart, Harry Rhodes and Jim Kirk form the group to the le front of the 4F 0-6-0.
E.R.Morten

(above). **Buxton, Staff.** Driver Bert Smart looks from the cab of an Ivatt 2-6-0 during shunting operations at Higher Buxton. *Courtesy D.Bradshaw*

Buxton MPD. Staff. Driver George Nadin (right), Firemen John Buxton, Terry Morson and Ron Heath feature in this photograph, they are standing at the side of the withdrawn former LNWR 0-8-0 No.**49348.** *Authors Collection*

Buxton Staff. The footplates of the 4F 0-6-0's were not exactly the last word in comfort, especially for the driver, who's perch was a small wooden board on top of the screw reverser, here, Derek Johnson is seen balancing on one of these contraptions aboard 4F No.**44059,** during a short break on the Sunday 'hopper banker' turn, during which seven I.C.I. hopper trains were banked from Tunstead to Peak Forest. *J.M. Bentley*

Buxton MPD. c.1961. Newly outshopped ex LNWR 0-8-0 No.**49446** provides the background for this cheerful group. From left to right they are : Fireman Terry Marshall, Peter Cooke, Driver Bob Bailey, and Firemen Sam Robinson, Tony Ratcliffe and Peter Barton. *J.M.Bentley*

Buxton Staff. c.1907/8. Although working days were long and arduous, time and energy was found for sports activities; three of the depot's teams appear in this set of pictures. Firstly, the Phillips Cup football team, all LNWR employees, circa 1907/08. Sadly, due to the passage of time, not many of the faces can now be identified, but amongst those who are known are : Players back row, far left, Jack Pickford, then come, Pearson, Latham, two more unknowns, then Mr Needham, Shed Master. Mr Hill Station Master is also in the line up. Players front row, far left, Walter Palfryman, second unknown, third Horace Hunt, fourth Bentley (drayman), G.Depledge, sixth unknown.   *Courtesy B.Palfryman*

Buxton Staff. c.1920s. The Buxton Railwaymen's Rifle Club, flourished for many years, and in this 1920s photograph, taken on the Midland station platform, the group, comprised of staff from both the Midland and LNWR sides, show off some of their trophies. Not all members of the party can be identified but those known are : Back row, far left, ex LNWR Driver Geo.Boulton, and next to him stands an ex Midland Railway Driver, Geo.Bryant, whilst on the far right is Booking Clerk Booth. The clerestory roofed carriage with its "Millers Dale" board heightens the 'period' atmosphere of the smartly attired group, as do, to their right, the drinking fountain and 'slot machines' one of which is of the type which almost certainly dispensed 'Nestles Chocolate'.
Courtesy J.Featherstone

L.M.S. (BUXTON) RIFLE CLUB.

Affiliated to the S.M.R.C. No. 36.
SEASON 1939.   MEMBERS' CARD.

M ....

President : Major B. Darbyshire, M.C., T.D.
Vice-Presidents :
His Worship the Mayor, Councillor J. W. Smith.
Lt.-Col. F. L. Parkin.   Alderman S. L. Pettitt.
Lt.-Col. E. Smalley.   W. L. Shipton, Esq.
Lt.-Col. H. Ruggard, R.E. Dr. R. W. Stewart.
Dr. G. C. Pether.   H. E. Reynolds, Esq.
Chairman : Mr. G. Bradshaw.
Vice-Chairman : Mr. A. S. Parker.
Committee :
Mr. J. Gregory, Mr. F. Boulton, Mr. G. Bryant,
Mr. J. Shufflebotham, Mr. C. Booth, Mr. J.
Brookes, Mr. G. Linaker, Mr. G. H. Thompson.
Captain : Mr. W. McQuire.
Vice-Captain : Mr. S. Brotherton.
Hon. Treasurer : Mr. A. S. Parker.
Hon. Secretary : Mr. S. Brotherton, "Allanton,"
Brown Edge Road.
Range Superintendent : Mr. W. McQuire.
Auditors : Mr. A. Barnfield, Mr. C. Booth.

Buxton Staff. The 'Late Twenties'. This photograph, taken in rural surroundings, is of the LNWR Depot's cricket team, some time between 1925-30. The members are: Back row, left to right, Frank Bagshaw, Reg Lomas, Arthur Buxton, Wilf Dakin, Jim Rickman and Eric Wilson. Middle Row, Herbert Bramwell, Harold Sigley and Charlie Blood. Front Row, Frank Mellor, Jim Lomas, Archie Clayton and Harry Whieldon.   *Courtesy Mrs A. Whieldon*

Buxton MPD. 22:06:65. Following the dieselisation of the Midland section expresses, work was found for 'Scots' and 'Jubilees', on such trains as the 8.00 am to Manchester Central and the 5.22 pm back, the engine standing spare at Trafford Park depot during the day time, ready to deputise in the event of any diesel engine failing on the St Pancras trains. The last regular 'named' engine to be used on this service was No.**45705** *Seahorse*, which was moved from Newton Heath to Trafford Park depot, although most of its time was spend at Buxton MPD. Shortly after No.**45705** commenced working the Buxton service one of its nameplates was stolen -the other was then removed for safety- this happened to many of the class. This, the first of two pictures, shows No.**45705** having its smokebox cleaned out by Fireman Denis Allerton. *J.M.Bentley*

Buxton MPD. August 1965. An attempt was made by two local youths, Ken Tyler and Peter Bentley to smarten *Seahorse* up, this included a clean-up and the fitting of two wooden replica nameplates, with which the locomotive ran, until a derailment at Trafford Park caused its withdrawal. This picture shows the engine in its 'smartened up' form. Following the removal of *Seahorse* from Buxton, Trafford Park supplied a 5MT 4-6-0 for the job until, such time as the the service was withdrawn. *J.M.Bentley*

Buxton MPD. 14:07:1964. By the mid 1960s, the express engines were disappearing very quickly, being unceremoniously bundled off to the scrapyards. Just one or two remained until the end and this nostalgic picture shows Royal Scot 4-6-0 No.**46155** *The Lancer*, having its tank refilled before working the 8.25 pm Mayfield parcels train from the former LNWR station at Buxton; this was the very last visit made by a Royal Scot class locomotive to Buxton. *J.M.Bentley*

Buxton MPD. 1964. LMS No.**44083**, a Buxton based locomotive brightened an evening for her crew, Driver Bunty Clayton and Fireman John Featherstone by dropping off the track as it approached the water tank; on examination the points over which she had just passed were found to be fitting correctly, so the mishap could only be put down to 'a mystery', for the crew it obviously happened at just the right place to 'leave it on the depot'.   *J.M.Bentley*

Buxton MPD. 16:10:1966 The removal of the old 'North Light' shed roof in the mid 1960s, and the replacement for half the length of the shed with a temporary covering, showed which way the future of the depot was heading. On this picture No.s.1 and 2 roads are closed, whilst the contractors remove the old roofing. The 350 hp diesel shunter stabled on the short No.6 road (right) was used for the Friden job, and shunting in the up sidings.   *J.M.Bentley*

Buxton Up Sidings. Date not known A group of sidings staff comprising Sam Smith, Yard Inspector, Ron Jones, Guard, and Sam Bellicoso, Shunter, stand at the side of the banking and shunting engine No.**48519**, driven by Bill Starkey.
Courtesy S.Bellicoso

Buxton MPD. 1967. One of the three ex Longmoor Military Railway, Stanier 2 8-0s, taken back into BR service in 1957-58, No.**48775**, numerically the las locomotive in the class, stands on the ashpit, with its crew, Driver Don Bradshav and Firemen Keith Chadwick.   *Courtesy D.Bradshav*

Buxton MPD. 1966
Sheltering beneath the temporary shed roof are shown some of the locomotives which provided the motive power for the depot in its last days, with examples of the Ivatt 2MT 2-6-0s, Stanier 8F 2-8-0s, and the former LNER J94 0-6-0 saddle tanks, transferred to Buxton following the closure of Rowsley depot, to work the Cromford and High Peak section; the pendant gas lights remained the only form of illumination until the building was finally demolished, and in the rafters above the nearest light is observed the running rail and travelling mechanism for a heavy duty lifting block.
J.M.Bentley

Buxton MPD. 1968. Following the closure of the depot on 4th March 1968, and the dieselisation of all remaining freight services, the demolition of the depot and its servicing plants was soon underway. The demolition, by explosives, of the coaling tower and water tank came as a great shock to many of the residents in Nunsfield Road and on Brown Edge, who were not only alarmed by the sound but, in many instances had their windows blown out or shattered by the blast as well.
D.Johnston

Buxton MPD. May 1968. The feeling of loss at the sad end of the depot was heightened later in the year by the arrival of a party of railway officials, who had come to explore the possibility of converting the old steam shed into a diesel depot as many of its facilities (only weeks earlier so wantonly destroyed), would have been of great value. What a surprise they had! They had no idea that the site had been cleared. The few diesels required to handle what was, then, the most minute amount of traffic left, were housed in the D.M.U. depot, which stood on the site of the first LNWR depot in the station yard. During a time of freight expansion, how useful the old depot, with its more than adequate room would have been. That's progress.
D.Johnston